Introductory Book

Advantage Meal Solutions Success Plan

2011 Edition

Stacey and Angela Davis

Stacey & Angela Davis
Advantage Meal Solutions
A division of Magic Meals Home Delivery LLC

Visit our websites at
www.AdvantageMeals.com
www.MealsLikeMagic.com

Printed in the United States of America
First Printing: January 8th 2011

Book Dedication

To our children, Evander and Marley - Our desire to experience life with you drove us to create our amazing lifestyle. We hope someday you look back on your childhood with the same amazement and wonder that we experience every day with you. Perhaps someday you will understand how blessed we were as a family to live and work together.

Disclaimer: – Because we live in the world we do

The way *lawyers* say it:

The way *we* say it:

You are responsible for your own decisions and their consequences. If you do not agree with this philosophy, please stop reading this book right now and do not purchase our business startup package! Without this philosophy of personal responsibility, you will not succeed.

Introductory Book

Advantage Meal Solutions
Success Plan

Table of Contents

The Advantage Meal Solutions Philosophy

We believe that food made with care and love is better than food made in a factory or a laboratory. We know that you should not eat food that contains ingredients made in a laboratory. We believe that our service makes our clients' lives both healthier and happier, and we take great pride and pleasure in that.

We believe that good food is the foundation of a good life. We believe in seeking locally grown, natural, and organic food and avoiding preservatives and chemicals when possible. We believe in eating a balanced and varied diet while enjoying, in moderation, those rich foods that bring you bliss.

We believe in working and living as a family. We include all of our family members in our work – whether it is household chores or work for our customers. Even our youngest child enjoys contributing by working in the garden and helping in the kitchen.

We believe in providing a high quality product and reliable service for our customers while building friendships that we hope will last a lifetime. And we believe that others who follow this philosophy will share our success and our pleasure in our work.

Stacey & Angela Davis

Forward

We fashioned this book to be an inexpensive and quick introduction to our Advantage Meal Success Plan. This book is for people who are considering starting their own meal solutions business. From this overview, you will be able to understand how our business works and get an idea of the effort and knowledge needed to be successful before you invest significant time and other resources into this self-employment opportunity.

First, we will share our family's story and how our dream was shaped by our own meal solutions business that we call Magic Meals. Through our personal dreams and experiences, we will help you understand what your business might look like. Then we will explain the business model—Advantage Meal Solutions—that can offer you this same dream.

This book is designed to be the first simple step in deciding if you want to invest your heart, soul, and financial resources in becoming self-employed by opening your own meal solutions business. If you decide that this business choice is not for you, then we are happy we helped you come to that conclusion with such a small investment of time and other resources. If, however, you decide to explore this business opportunity further then we are here to help you on your journey.

We have broken the details of our Success Plan into a number of affordable books and resources. This book introduces the concept of a meal solutions business. The next book, *By the Numbers*, opens our financial records to you. We share what it cost us to open our business, how we price our services, and what we make. At the end of *By the Numbers*, you will have the information you need to decide if you want to proceed in the pursuit of self-employment as a meal solutions business owner.

If you decide to open your own business, we have collected everything we use in the operation of our successful meal solutions business into specific and affordable blocks of information. The idea for these blocks is to allow you to pick and choose where you need assistance and not be forced to purchase information that you already have access to. Those blocks are outlined at the end of each book.

Our goal is to give *you* all the advantages we wish *we* had when we started our business six years ago. The meal solution business is not for everyone, but for the right people we know it can transform their lives and communities, because it has already transformed ours.

Now it is time to get to work.

"If one advances confidently in the direction of his dreams, and endeavors to live the life which he has imagined, he will meet with a success unexpected in common hours."

Henry David Thoreau

Introduction

Seven years ago, we considered our family's future. We did not want to raise children while stuck in jobs that would give us little quality time together – as a couple and even less with the children we planned. We yearned for a better way of *making* a living while actually *living*. We decided that we needed our own business to both provide materially for our family and at the same time occupy us with rewarding and fulfilling work. We found that business, and after the struggles and the joys of making it a success, we are eager to share it with you.

Our family provides assistance to those in our community who need regular or occasional help with meal planning and preparation. Our service helps people eat healthy, home-cooked meals in the comfort of their own home. Our home-based business has done wonders for our community while providing a lifestyle for our family that once seemed nearly unobtainable.

We work as much or as little as we choose, with the sure knowledge that when we choose to work less, we are also choosing to make less money. We work at the times of our choosing, often taking the afternoon hours for household chores or family pastimes. Our family now has the freedom we only fantasized about in the past.

We no longer dread work. Instead, our entire family feels good about what we do and we take pride in knowing that we are truly helping our neighbors. Our service has helped hundreds of  individuals learn that healthy meals can also be enjoyable meals. Our meals provide senior citizens in our community with a valuable resource to help them stay independent in their own homes. We provide simple solutions for people with medically restrictive diets, and we have helped hundreds of families through their most difficult times by providing tasty, healthy meals when they were needed most. We grow a large organic garden, and use much of that produce for our client's meals. What our family's garden cannot provide we strive to buy from other local producers. By buying locally, we support our community's local producers and farmer's markets.

The timing for starting your own Advantage Meal Solutions business could not be better. Faced with troubled economic times, people are actively looking for the solutions our business offers. Each week we have new clients contacting us searching for affordable alternatives to expensive diets, takeout food, and dining out. People facing the financial burden of assisted living, the medical expenses related to obesity and diabetes, or the financial necessity of longer work hours find solutions to their mealtime struggles with our services. Advantage Meal Solutions simplifies people's lives.

Through years of trial and error, we have developed an affordable and accessible plan for business success. Now we are offering everything we have learned and everything we use to run our successful business to you at a very affordable price. We know that this business plan is the opportunity that many of you are seeking. The detailed business plan and comprehensive operational procedures included in the Success Plan will trim years off your learning curve and greatly increase your chance of success. Unlike so many who take the plunge to self-employment, you will begin your business armed with a tested and proven plan, procedures, and marketing materials. Instead of reinventing the wheel, you will begin your years of self-employment with almost all of the advantages that our established business enjoys today! If you start your business with a strong work ethic and honest character, the growth potential of your new home-based business is almost unlimited.

Experts tell us that only one in three new small businesses will succeed. Of those successful businesses, it takes most three years to break even.

Experts also agree that franchises have a much higher rate of success than businesses started without experienced guidance. Unfortunately, franchise opportunities are most often too expensive for the fledgling entrepreneur, leaving many people without that option.

We know that you can beat the odds. We know this because we did it, and we did it without the advantages that you will have when you start your business using the Advantage Success Plan. Our family has made a comfortable living after starting with very little money. So can yours.

We sincerely believe that our family is offering you the best of all worlds. We are sharing nearly all of the benefits of a franchise without the costs associated with one. Why would we do this? Simply stated, our lifestyle is more important to us than our income. Keeping track of your business and its sales, in order to collect a percentage of your earnings, sounds to us faintly unscrupulous and very tedious. Instead, we offer you everything we have learned - our recipes, our brochures and flyers, and our support - for a modest one-time investment of less than two thousand dollars. You can be in business – up and running in just weeks - for a total investment of as little as three thousand dollars! With hard work and an approachable and outgoing personality, you can have your startup expenses completely recovered in a matter of months.

Before you make that decision, however, you need to know more about the business model and the people offering it to you. First, we will share our story and our vision of the future with you. As you learn more about our family and our dreams, we think that many of you will find our story is much like your own.

"All adventures, especially into new territory, are scary."

Sally Ride

Past, Present, and Future

The Journey

Today we are at a great place in our business and personal life. We have a level of control over our work and home life that most people long for, but few ever really obtain.

Getting to where we are now was not a perfectly linear—or even a particularly rational—process. It was a voyage of discovery—discovery not just of business truths, but of truths about ourselves. Understanding what we needed and wanted out of a business was the first step to creating, and ultimately to enjoying, those things.

The first part of our journey was discovery. Not just discovery of a great business model—that came second, actually—but self-discovery. And we are not by any means at the end of our journey—personal or business.

We will spend some time in this chapter reliving the first parts of this journey with you. This will help you see how we got where we are, and how we plan to get where we want to be. We hope this will help you on your own journey toward greater freedom and self-reliance.

Beginning the Search

Seven years ago, we began our search for a business that we could start ourselves without much capital and without borrowing too much. We had a background in being self-employed, having owned and operated a small chain of retail stores. We learned much about being self-employed during those years. One of the lasting lessons was the awareness that we never wanted to be shackled to a retail store again. With that lesson as the first criteria, we narrowed our search for our new family business to home-based opportunities only.

Defining What We Wanted

Actually, we developed a whole list of criteria for our new business.

- Home-based
- Work that we both enjoy
- Kid friendly, allowing us to work with our children much of the time
- Time-flexible so that we can raise our own kids without relying on outside childcare
- Something that helps people rather than just filling their lives with more junk and debt
- Capable of employing both of us full-time so we would not have to choose which of us would remain trapped in a traditional job

while the other stayed home with our
children and business

Over the next few days we created a comically
untidy list of our passions. We then limited our list
to those interests that we shared, and sorted them
into groups that demonstrated some potential for
synergy. One group of shared passions stood out:

- Good, yet healthy, food
- Cooking
- Cooking for other people
- Foods made from the least processed
  ingredients available

It was clear from this exercise that we would both
enjoy a business centered on food. The obvious
choice was to open a restaurant. However, a
restaurant certainly did not fit our list of criteria.
Actually, it violated at least half—and possibly
more—of the criteria! Therefore, a restaurant was
entirely out of the question. We kept searching for a
business model that met our requirements.

The Answer, or at Least an Answer

After months of research, we decided to explore the
idea of making our living as personal chefs. A
personal chef is a cook who prepares meals for a
client in the client's home kitchen, based upon the
client's needs and personal preferences. This
business model was the best we had found so far. It

had time flexibility, no retail location, the ability to run all base operations from home, and limited startup costs. While not as kid friendly as we had dreamed, it had potential for children to join us on select cook days. It was definitely a service that people needed. The traditional personal chef business model was not the perfect home business for us, but it made a good place to start.

At the time, personal chef services were very popular on the coasts but uncommon in the central part of the country where we live. While neither of us had formal chef training, we were both skilled "grandma taught" cooks. Since we lived in the heartland, we decided that we could be successful as personal chefs by providing home-style versions of fancy foods.

Decision made, we started the first incarnation of our home-based business, Magic Meals Personal Chefs. We began our business with a modest investment of $3,000, which included a membership in a national personal chef association. We already owned some of the things we needed for our new business: we had a car, a personal computer, some cookware, and some presentable casual clothes to wear during our cook days.

We focused all of our energy on growing our new business. We had the enormous advantage of having years of small business marketing experience. In those first few months, we used every low-cost and no-cost marketing trick we knew to find clients for our fledgling business.

Within the first year, we had grown our business to the point that we could both quit our day jobs. Our new business was now providing a decent living with much of the flexibility that we desired. We were successful, or so we thought.

Taking Off: Evolution Through Necessity

What we did not know was that this first food business was only the starting point. As we went about growing our business, we were ever watchful for new opportunities and a better way to grow our dream. As we integrated each new opportunity into our business, we found that Magic Meals was beginning to evolve. In the next few years, our food business would transform into something larger and more rewarding than we had dared to imagine as we began the journey.

The traditional personal chef business model focuses on marketing to affluent professionals who do not have time or interest in cooking for themselves. As we started our business, we followed this traditional focus. We marketed aggressively (yet very inexpensively) to our small city's most successful families. While we had early success with our business, we soon found that the traditional personal chef business model had some significant downsides. Our original business had too small of a client base, it was too difficult to market, and it was nearly impossible to maintain a steady cash flow. Equally important for our family, it was not as rewarding as we had hoped.

Opportunity From Unexpected Quarters

However, we soon found unexpected opportunities that would shape our new business in profound ways. Through referrals, blind luck, and the necessity born of slow cash flow periods, we stumbled into cooking for a handful of folks who sincerely needed our service. These unanticipated clients had an intense impact on how we viewed our role in our community. While we know these new clients believed that our service changed their lives for the better, we are not sure that they will ever fully appreciate how deeply they touched our lives and influenced the direction of our business.

The Elderly - Joe

Our first unexpected client was Joe, a very nice man of modest means who was well over ninety years old. Joe simply wanted to stay in his own home. It was a simple wish that grew more difficult each year.

His children, scattered around the country and unable to directly assist him, found us on the internet. Joe had access to a state sponsored meals-on-wheels program, but that service was not available for evening or weekend meals. The children were happy to help pay for our service as it represented the gift of independence for their father. They found that our service not only allowed their father to stay in his own home, but was considerably less expensive than assisted living options available.

For us, Joe was more than a client, he was a part of our mission: this elderly man really needed us and it felt good to help him. He loved having our young family—complete with new baby—visit his home while we cooked, and we came to think of him as part of our extended family. Cooking for him was difficult at first, though. Many of our recipes needed to be dramatically modified to appeal to his aging taste buds. We also learned to recreate many of the dishes that he missed from the days when his wife was still at his side.

It was while cooking for Joe that we first discovered how rewarding our business could be. His not-so-unique situation challenged us to rethink our business and our role in our community. Long after he was forced from his home by a hard fall, his influence on our lives remains. This one man opened our eyes to a quickly growing segment of our population that is in desperate need of meal solutions.

Diet Management - Kathy

The next remarkable step in our business transformation came when we began cooking for a woman who needed to lose a lot of weight. Kathy had been heavy all of her adult life. She had tried every conceivable diet, and she failed each time. She knew that someday her weight would be, quite literally, the death of her. She had read all the books and understood how to eat for health. Kathy's problem was that she did not have the physical ability and skills to assure that she had the right food available at the right time. She also did not have the willpower to limit the portion sizes of her meals for long enough for healthy eating to become ingrained as habit. So she turned to us for help.

Once again we reinvented our recipes, menus, and packaging (for better portion control) to meet her not-so-unique needs. Soon Kathy began experiencing the sustainable weight loss success she had only dreamed of before. She was ecstatic and we were so happy to be a part of her success. Once again, a phone call from one person brought into focus another growing segment of our population that needed the meal solutions we could offer.

Special Medical Needs - Carla

Our next business revelation came from a referral from an existing client who recommended that her sister, Carla give us a call. The sister, Carla, had just been diagnosed with celiac disease, which requires a gluten-free diet. She had never really cooked for herself, and she was terribly ill. She desperately needed to find a way to get reliable gluten-free meals while she learned to live with her new medically restricted diet. We pored over the information provided by her doctor, and researched for days before finally telling her that we could provide the meal solutions she needed.

We cooked all of her meals for over six months. During that time, we were invited to speak by a local celiac support group, and we soon had nearly a dozen celiac patients that we cooked for once a month. As medical professionals learned of our service, we began getting referrals for other clients on medically restricted clients, including those with heart disease, on dialysis, and many more conditions with special dietary needs. Once again, a completely new market emerged for our meal solutions.

In time we came to the full realization that our meal service did not need to be marketed to just the affluent professional crowd. We discovered that instead we could make a comfortable living cooking for people who sincerely needed what we could provide. With our new paradigm, we set about inventing a completely new business model.

Putting it All Together

First, we modified and standardized our menus to keep meal costs as low as possible while still meeting the needs of our new clients. As we struggled to find a balance between affordability for our customers and a comfortable living for our family, we continued to adjust pricing, packaging, menus, and services. We experimented with new meal packages, new menus, new recipes, and new packaging. Through trial and error, we finally created a meal system that meets our clients' needs and still gives us the predictability to be able to control costs and make our business a sustainable way of life for our family.

During this time, we also tested a wide array of low-cost marketing techniques and strategies to reach our new target audiences. As we found techniques that worked, we refined our message and branding to effectively reach our less well-to-do clientele. Our brochures and business cards became more focused in message and found the proper balance between the appearance of professionalism and affordability. Soon our marketing graduated to community partnerships and events as well as the more obvious radio and television advertising. Every step of the way, we dodged the advice of the people who were trying to sell us their advertising services. In the end, we created and refined our own low-cost yet effective alternative advertising plan that has seen our business thrive and grow with a very small marketing budget.

Soon our little business was rapidly growing. While we still cooked for a handful of people who simply chose not to cook for themselves, most of our new clients were people who were unable to cook for themselves. Soon people started giving our meal service as a gift to friends and family facing the most difficult times of their lives. We cooked for people facing serious illness, those who had lost a loved one, and those who were learning to live with a new baby in the house.

We now had a vision of what our business was destined to become, and it was not the traditional personal chef business. Our business was evolving into something exciting, innovative, and as large as we chose to let it become. Instead of cooking for a very small niche market of the wealthiest people in town, we were now offering our services to everyone in our city unable to cook their own meals. Our niche market had grown much larger.

Now we had more clients than we could cook for by taking our equipment to each client's home. To allow our meal solutions business to grow we needed a kitchen. While having a dedicated kitchen quickly became our goal, it was delayed while we saved our money to be able to do so without taking on substantial debt.

Into the Present

We continued to save our pennies and dollars while we looked for the perfect location for our business. Two years after we started Magic Meals, we moved our home-based business into a larger home in a nicer area. We found a great house in the country, with a few acres and a second, rudimentary kitchen in the walkout basement. It was the perfect setup for us. We remodeled the second kitchen in the most affordable ways possible and had it licensed by the state. We then began cooking from home and delivering frozen meals to our clients. The flexibility this setup offered us was amazing. Not only could we care for our toddler son in our own home while working, but we were no longer limited to cooking for only one client per day. Now we had the capacity to serve our emerging client base.

We once again began transforming our recipes, menus, services, and procedures to allow us to cook for multiple clients on a single menu. This made our cook days more efficient and profitable.

We also revisited our marketing strategies and procedures. Sales calls that used to require an in-home consultation to secure a new client could now be done by telephone and email. We streamlined our online message and created weekly menu emails. We set procedures for taking calls from potential new clients. We developed phone techniques and scripts that made new client calls less stressful by making them nearly guaranteed sales.

Our new home-based kitchen allowed our business to offer smaller meal packages while still increasing our profit margin. Soon we were cooking for a dozen or more clients each week.

With our own licensed kitchen, we discovered that we had even more work flexibility. Most weeks we shopped and cooked Monday through Wednesday, and delivered Thursday and Friday. Other times we might have plans during the week so we would choose to cook Saturday through Monday, take a few days off, and then deliver on Friday. When the weather was nice, we often decided to cook in the early morning and late evening, and keep our days open to play outside with the kids.

We were a bit surprised that with the larger scale of our business came widespread appreciation for our new business model. We began getting calls and emails every month from people around the country who wanted to have a home-based business much like ours. At first, we tried to spend time with each person, answering his or her questions and sharing our experience. Soon, however, answering every call for assistance was simply overwhelming. We did not have the time or energy to start from scratch with every person who called. That is when we began exploring the idea of collecting all of our meal solutions experience into a single package. We reasoned that if we had a single collection of business startup information, we could help more people with a lower impact on our own family time.

To accomplish this, we have spent the time we would have devoted to helping only a few people to, instead, gather and prepare our extensive resources. Those resources include this book the remainder of the Advantage Success Plan. We are so excited about the advantages we are now able to offer those who call us for help to start a business similar to our own. If we had access to this success plan when we started our business, we could have saved years of trial-and-error learning.

Moving Forward
Today our business, Magic Meals Home Delivery, continues to thrive and is once again on the cusp of

transforming into something larger. The only way to scale up from our current business model is to no longer do all of the work ourselves. If we want to continue to grow our capacity, we are going to have to hire others to help with some of the shopping, cooking, cleanup, and delivery. We are still weighing the advantages and disadvantages of allowing our business to grow to this scale.

The major advantage to this larger scale is the ability to serve more clients while maintaining our own work schedule freedom. The disadvantages include increased overhead and operations complexity. While we are blessed to have the background of having larger workforces in our retail experience, we still have not decided if this is the right choice for our lives. This is a very difficult decision for our family. We really feel that our service is helping the people of our community. We want to be able to help as many as possible. Therefore, we have some thinking to do about any further expansion. Regardless of our final decision, we will share our research and insight about this larger scale in the Advantage Success Plan.

Sharing the Dream

We do know, however, that by offering you the opportunity to copy and improve upon our business model we can still achieve our dream of helping more people. By giving you the advantage of our five years of experimentation, learning, and growth, we know that you will have the opportunity to hit the ground running. You could be providing meal solutions to your community within weeks of receiving your Advantage Success Plan. With our shared success, our network of family owned businesses could be serving every city in America in a few short years. We dream of a world where every city in America has at least one highly visible family business like ours to counter the glut of fast-food restaurant chains. If you share that dream with us, together we can change our world.

"Thousands of candles can be lit from a single candle, and the life of the candle will not be shortened. Happiness never decreases by being shared."

Hindu Prince Gautama Siddharta

How Advantage Meal Solutions Works

Our business provides meal solutions for those who cannot cook for themselves. We serve people who are searching for meal solutions to simplify their lives or the life of someone they love. Through years of trial-and-error, we have found a balance between an entirely customized service and bulk service that not only meets the needs of our clients but makes our business model both rewarding and sustainable. We have created a seven-week rotation of menus and recipes that meets the needs of the vast majority of our clients, while allowing us the predictability to be able to run our business in a fiscally responsible manner. We also offer customized menus to address some of the most unusual diet requirements introduced by new customers.

The Basics of the Service

As we discussed before and explore in greater depth in the next chapter, our Meal Solutions Success Plan can operate in three distinct sizes or scales. In all three scales, we provide the same basic service to our clients. This consistency is paramount to the Advantage Success Plan since this allows you to start your business at the smallest scale with a very affordable investment, and naturally mature into the larger scales.

Regardless of scale, our meal solutions service offers four basic types of meal plans, which we discuss in greater depth below. These types are:

- Senior Meals
- Medically Restricted Diets
- Weight Loss Meals
- Short Term Meal Solutions

Each of these meal plans include ingredients, recipes, portions, and packaging to meet the general goals of clients who fall within these categories. Each of these basic plans are then customized to take into account personal taste and individualized goals.

Before we discuss the meal plans, we will talk about our basic principles of ingredient selection, menu planning, meal preparation, and packaging.

Ingredient Selection

All of our meals are prepared using the best available ingredients. We proudly tell our clients that we will not feed them anything we would not feed our own children, and we are very selective about their diet. All of our meals feature local and natural ingredients when practical. We find that our clients are very receptive to the idea that local food is better food. They are not only accepting, but excited about the prospect of having their food dollars support local farmers and the local economy. Not only have we found that offering local ingredients when possible leads to good food, but it also leads to good marketing. We feature the idea of local ingredients in our brochures, flyers, website, and email menu. We share all of these marketing resources in the Advantage Success Plan so you can use our work as the basis of your marketing plan.

Our recipes also feature whole grains, lean meats, and good fats. Our clients can also count on our meals to be low in sodium and without preservatives. Our commitment to holistic health is very important to the vast majority of our clients and one of our major selling points.

We do the much of our grocery shopping at normal grocery stores and club style stores. While it would be cheaper to do more of our shopping through wholesale food distributors, the inconsistent quality and often overly processed foods found there is a compromise we are not willing to make for our customers and friends. During the summer months, we grow much of the fresh produce we use in our business. We also purchase a significant portion of it from other local producers. For us, supporting local family farms is worth the extra cost and our clients tell us that it is important to them as well.

Menu Planning

All of our menus feature recipes that are healthy versions of home-style favorites that follow the American Heart Association and the American Diabetes Association recommendations for healthy diets. We take pride in teaching our customers that good food can also be good tasting food. Our recipes feature whole grains, good fats, and lots of vegetables.

Through the years, our database of recipes that we use regularly has been revised and focused to now only include about fifty tried and true recipes. These recipes make up the core of the menus that we offer our clients in all scales of our business.

We use an inexpensive database software package to manage our recipes and client menus. The software not only generates a shopping list, but also tracks our client's likes and dislikes. The software saves us hours of work each week and provides an easy way to manage all of the details needed to makes our business run smoothly. There are a number of such software packages available, and in Advantage Success Plan, we make specific recommendations on the package that we have found performs best in our business model, and give you advice on how to best utilize this important business tool.

All of our core recipes are included in the success plan in both hard copy and digital format to be easily imported into the database menu planning software that we recommend.

Meal Preparation

Our commitment to healthy yet tasty food continues throughout meal preparation. Not only do we carefully monitor the types and amounts of cooking fats we add to our dishes, we stress food safety in every stage of our production. This includes proper washing and preparation of fresh produce, good meat handling procedures, proper cooking temperatures, and proper cooling and packaging techniques. Through years of study, we are comfortable with the food safety procedures that we share in the Advantage Success Plan. The details in our success plan will also help you find local resources to hone your own food safety skills.

Packaging

Our meals are packaged to meet the needs of our clients. We can package our meals in single servings or combined servings to feed a family of two or more. We offer both full size portions and smaller portions for those who need portion control to achieve their weight goals. These same smaller portions are very popular with many of our senior clients with small appetites. Most of our clients prefer that we use tray packaging that allows the entrees and side dishes to be reheated together. We have finally found an inexpensive and simple tray packaging system that we use in our own business. We share the details of this system in the Advantage Success Plan.

Usually, when we provide meals for an entire family, we package the entrée and sides separately—making warming of family sized meals much easier. Many families find that our meal solutions are their only real opportunity to sit down together for dinner at home without the hours of planning, shopping, cooking, and cleanup.

"The only thing that will stop you from fulfilling your dreams is you"

Tom Bradley

Advantage Meal Solutions

Now that you understand the basic principles of our meal service, we will explore the types of meal plans in more detail. While our Meal Solutions business can help anyone who calls, we concentrate on four general areas of need and our meal plans are designed for these groups.

Senior Meals

Designed for our senior citizen clients who are striving to remain independent in their own homes, this meal plan is crafted for their unique needs and tastes. Like all of our meals, the senior meals focus on healthy versions of foods that these elders recognize and love. We have designed the recipes found in this meal plan to be full flavored, low sodium offerings that are high in fiber, higher in moisture content for easier chewing and to help maintain hydration in our seniors, and tend toward natural and healthy sweets to appeal to their aging taste buds. Most of these meals are packaged in smaller portions to match a smaller senior appetite. The Senior Meal Plan is very popular and makes up about half of our meals.

Weight Loss Meals

This meal plan is our second most popular offering. These portion-controlled meals provide healthy and satisfying food to help our clients meet their weight loss goals. Most diets fail, and they do so because the dieter does not have the right food available at the right time. Our meals solve that problem. We offer our weight loss meals in two packaging options— traditional meals and what we call Grab & Go Meals. The Grab & Go Meals are single dish meals that are designed to be eaten on the go by our busiest clients.

These small meals are specifically designed to replace the fast food lines that so many of us fall prey to. Most of our weight loss clients get a combination of traditional meals and Grab & Go meals each month, thus assuring that they will always have the right food at the right time.

Short Term Meal Solutions

These meal packages make the perfect gift when someone is facing life's most challenging times.

Offices and families often go in together to provide meals for new parents, a loved one facing a prolonged illness or death in the family, and many other difficult situations. Our gift clients find that a month's worth of home-cooked meals provide comfort long after flowers would be wilted and gone. Many of our gift clients become long-term clients, so not only is this Meal Plan a profitable niche market, but it becomes another valuable marketing tool.

Medically Restricted Meals

These meals are the most challenging and rewarding portion of our business. We do not prescribe any form of diet or meal plan. Instead, we carefully prepare these meals following guidelines provided by the individual client's medical provider. Some of these guidelines are so simple that they easily fit within our normal meal plans. For example, all of our meals follow the general guidelines from the American Diabetes Association and most of our diabetic clients have found success when they learn to eat the portion controlled balanced meals that we provide. Other medically restricted diets are much more difficult to follow. For example, celiac patients cannot have any gluten. This requires special ingredients and special procedures. Through years of working with medical professionals, we have compiled a list of resources to help new Meal Solutions business owners meet the needs of their most desperate clients. Each Meal Solutions business owner will need to find his or her own comfort level with each medically restricted diet. There are some diets we just do not offer, as we are not comfortable that we can safely meet the needs of clients on these diets. For those that we do serve, this is a lucrative and rewarding portion of our business model.

Through years of experimentation, we have found that these four areas of focus encompass nearly all of the people who call or email for our assistance. By narrowing our marketing to these areas, we have created a much more concise advertising message that can effectively and efficiently reach our target audience.

"[Magic Meals] is a terrific service! They make eating right simple and fun by developing a balanced, healthy menu based upon your own food preferences. For someone who oft takes the easy way out of cooking (pizza, anyone?), being able to pop a pre-planned meal in the oven for a few minutes is a tremendous convenience."

Tomorrow

That is our story. You now know who we are, where we started, and where we are now. The question is;

Can you imagine yourself in a similar story?

If the answer is yes, then tomorrow you should do some more research. Look around your community and see who needs a little help with their everyday meals to make their lives just a little better. See who your business will be competing with. Is there anything even close to a meal solutions business in your town? Do they offer good, healthy food and professional service? Do they nurture stronger community and healthier individuals?

When you're ready, order the second book that is about twice as long as this little booklet. That short book, called *By the Numbers*, gives you access to nearly all of our data and finances. You'll also find out about the different possible scales for your meal solutions business, how to identify your potential clients, how much it will cost you to open your business, and how much money you might be able to make in your new business.

Some individuals and families with a very strong self-employment experience have started their meal solutions business with just the *By the Numbers* book. However, most have chosen to gain every possible advantage by also selecting portions of the Advantage Success Plans Blocks. There you will find the details you need to plan, open, operate, and grow your meal solutions business.

As for our family, tomorrow we will continue to live our dream. Our biggest challenge these days is deciding how to allow our business to grow. For us, it's not about volume but quality of life for our family. How big do we want to get? How busy is too busy? That's a choice we'll have to make tomorrow…and when we know the answer that is right for our family business, we'll share it with you.

Advantage Meals Success Plan

Below is an outline of the resources we have to offer. You'll see that some are available immediately and others are in process. Please check online at www.AdvantageMeals.com to see changes in availability and pricing.

Introductory Books	Price	Availability
The Introductory Book (this book)	$9 PDF $15 Print	PDF & Print In Stock
Meal Solutions By the Numbers – Gets into the details of how our business runs and how yours might look. Helps you figure out how much starting your business will cost and how much you might be able to make.	$29 PDF $40 Print	PDF & Print In Stock

Advantage Success Plan Blocks		
Business Setup Block	$300	NYA
Business Branding and Marketing Block	$400	PDF In Stock
Final Business Startup Block	$300	NYA
Operations Block	$300	PDF In Stock
Growing Business Block	$300	NYA

We also have a number or resources planned for the future. These include:

- Website Development and Hosting
- Improved menu / client software
- Additional Recipe Packages
- Online based network for sharing of resources.

Epilogue: Stacey's Dream

This book was co-written by Stacey and Angela. One evening after most of it was complete Stacey found himself in a dreamy mood after a nice day with the family and he was moved to write down his musings.

I have a dream. Perhaps it is crazy dream, but maybe it will succeed. Maybe, we will change the world.

The dream began so simply…

I once dreamed that we could create a successful home-based business that would allow us to stay at home with our kids while earning enough to support our family. *I know this is possible because we have done it.*

I once dreamed that a local business could thrive by providing healthy home-cooked meals to the people in our community who most needed assistance. *I know this is possible because we have done it.*

I once dreamed that I could own a business in which I took great pride knowing that my community was better off because my business existed. *I know this is possible because we have done it.*

Yet I still dream…

I dream that my family and I can share our success and dreams in such a way that people will witness our passion and sincerity.

I dream that 100,000 people will listen when we speak from our hearts about our home-based business and how it changed our lives and could change theirs.

I dream that those people will be inspired by the possibility of what we might achieve together and each will decide to tell our story to just 10 more people.

I dream that each of those people will tell 10 more people how a network of locally owned businesses with shared dreams is changing their communities for the better.

I dream that a mere 1% of the people who hear our story will find that they share our passions and dreams and be moved to read the introductory books where we lay open our hearts, souls, and financial records to allow them to find out if they want to own and operate a business like ours.

I dream that 10% of those who read our books will decide that they want to be self-employed following the Advantage Meal Solutions Success Plan.

I dream that 80% of those new businesses will be successful when supported by the Advantage Success Plan and a network of like-minded meal solution businesses.

It is just a dream. If we achieve it, we will have 8,000 locally owned family businesses spread across the United States of America creating an alliance of businesses destined to change our world. Each of these family businesses will be providing a basic service to help those in their community who most need help. Each of these businesses will be committed to doing business in such a way to support local food and the local economy. Each will be committed to building a network of small, locally owned businesses that strive together to create a staggering collective marketing effort that will allow them to undertake television, radio, and internet advertising campaigns on par with the best offered by industrial agriculture and franchise restaurants. This network of entrepreneurial families will combine their collective influence and resources to save on business supplies, insurance, and possibly even to influence government policy. They will change the world.

Can We?

Can my family and yours change the way America allows their elders to age?

Can my family and yours change the obesity trends in America?

Can my family and yours change how American families sit down to supper?

Can my family and yours resurrect the American family farm?

Can my family and yours save your local economy?

Yes, we can.

It is a big dream. A crazy big dream. But when we consider each small step, each step seems reasonable. If each step is reasonable, then mustn't the dream be reasonable as well?

Why not? It begins when your family joins mine.

Angela and I have already taken the first steps in the Dream.

Will you take the next step?

Share the Dream

Regardless of whether the time is right for you to become self-employed, you can still be part of the dream by helping to tell our story. To grow this network of locally owned family business, we need your help.

Do you have friends or family who share your passions and dreams? Do you know someone who has been searching for a better way of life? Perhaps someone you know became unemployed in these difficult economic times. If so, please consider taking this opportunity to share the dream and, perhaps, change their lives while helping advance the dream of the Advantage Meal Solutions network of locally owned businesses. When finished with this book pass it along to them, or buy them a copy of their own as a gift. Your gift could be the gift of self-employment.

Even if you do not know a specific person you believe might be ready for a Meal Solutions Business, you can still help spread the dream.

Write an email to your friends telling them about this family in Kansas who thinks they can change the world with a network of locally owned family businesses that provide meal solutions in their communities.

Write a letter to the editor of your local newspaper.

Post a link to The Advantage Meal Solutions' website on your Facebook or MySpace account.

Take your copy of this book to your local club.

Call your local radio or television show that sometimes has on guests and recommend that they contact us.

Invite us to your event to speak. If we can afford the trip and schedule it with our family and business, we will be there.

If you have other ideas and need our help, please do not hesitate to contact us.

Also, if you have suggestions or corrections to this book, please contact us. We are printing this book on-demand, which means that we can and will make updates and changes at anytime.

Once again, thank you for your time and thank you for sharing the dream.

Stacey and Angela Davis

Advantage Meal Solutions
Attn: Stacey & Angela Davis
6722 SW Urish Road
Auburn, KS 66402

785-727-5495
Contact@AdvantageMeals.com
www.AdvantageMeals.com

www.ingramcontent.com/pod-product-compliance
Lightning Source LLC
Chambersburg PA
CBHW021927170526
45157CB00005B/2221